THE MUSEUM OF THE CITY OF NEW YORK
Portraits of America

Bridges of
New York City

THE MUSEUM OF THE CITY OF NEW YORK
Portraits of America

Bridges of New York City

Cara A. Sutherland

BARNES
&NOBLE
BOOKS
NEW YORK

A BARNES & NOBLE BOOK

© 2003 by Barnes & Noble Publishing, Inc.

Library of Congress Cataloging-in-Publication Data

Sutherland, Cara A.
    Bridges of New York City / Cara A. Sutherland
        p. cm. -- (Portraits of America)
    Includes bibliographical references.
    ISBN 0-7607-3885-8
    1. Bridges--New York (State)--New York--Pictorial works. 2. Bridges--New York (State)--New York--History. I. Title. II. Series.

    TG25.N5 S88 2002
    624'.2'097471--dc21

                                                    2002033934

Editor: Hallie Einhorn
Art Director: Jeff Batzli
Designer: Lynne Yeamans
Photography Editor: Janice Ackerman
Production Manager: Richela Fabian Morgan

Color separations by Bright Arts Graphics (S) Pte Ltd.
Printed and bound in China by C&C Offset Printing Co. Ltd.

10 9 8 7 6 5 4 3 2 1

About the Museum of the City of New York

The Museum of the City of New York is one of New York City's great cultural treasures—the first U.S. museum dedicated to the study of a single city. Founded in 1923, it presents the nearly four hundred–year evolution of one of history's most important metropolises through exhibitions, educational programs, and publications, and by collecting and preserving the artifacts that tell New York's remarkable stories.

The Museum's collection of 1.5 million objects reflects the diverse and dramatic history of New York City. In addition to prints and photographs, the Museum collects and preserves paintings and sculptures, costumes, theater memorabilia, decorative arts and furniture, police and fire fighting materials, toys made or used in New York, material related to the history of the port, and thousands of varied objects and documents that illuminate the lives of New Yorkers, past and present. Among the gems of the collections are gowns worn at George Washington's inaugural ball, New York's last surviving omnibus and one of its last Checker Cabs, archives of the work of renowned photographers Jacob A. Riis and Berenice Abbott, the world's largest collection of Currier & Ives prints, and pieces of the Times Square news "zipper."

Through its Department of Learning, the Museum offers programs to thousands of teachers and students from all five boroughs every year, including guided tours, teacher training, and its annual New York City History Day contest—the nation's largest urban history fair. Other activities for audiences of all ages include hands-on workshops, performances, book readings, scholarly conferences and lectures, films, and walking tours.

The Museum's rich collections and archives are available to the public for research. To learn how to explore the collections or how to order reproductions of images, visit the Museum's website at www.mcny.org. The website also features exhibition previews, up-to-date program information, an on-line Museum shop, virtual exhibitions, student aids, and information on how you can support the Museum's work.

MUSEUM OF THE
CITY OF NEW YORK
1220 Fifth Avenue
New York, NY 10029
(212) 534-1672
www.mcny.org

Contents

Above: The Brooklyn Bridge is one of the most recognizable bridges in the United States. In this circa 1894 photograph, pedestrians stroll across the span.

INTRODUCTION

Crossing the Rivers

"No man is an island, entire of itself; every man is a piece of the continent, a part of the main." What English poet John Donne wrote in 1623 about the individual's place in society can be applied to a city's relationship with its environment. Linkage is important, if not crucial, for social and economic survival. Consider the situation of New York City. For the most part, it exists as an archipelago. Of the five boroughs, only the Bronx is connected to the mainland of New York State. Manhattan, Brooklyn, Queens, and Staten Island all depend upon bridges to connect them with one another and the world at large.

New York's earliest settlers—native and European—faced the challenge of crossing the rivers that shape the island now known as Manhattan. On the west is the mighty Hudson River, which begins as a stream far north in the Adirondack Mountains and grows to a width of 4,400 feet (1,341m) at its mouth in Upper New York Bay. Running parallel to the Hudson at the northeast end of the island is the Harlem River, which flows into the eastern water border known as the East River. These three rivers surround the island, linking it to the interior and the Atlantic Ocean. The English explorer Henry Hudson is known for his travels in the area. Arriving in New York Harbor on September 2, 1609, Hudson would document these waterways, helping to pave the way for European settlement and the creation of the colony of New Netherland in 1614. The Dutch West India Company would be formed in 1621, and several years later, in 1624, the first families would arrive at Fort Orange, located near present-day Albany.

In 1626, Peter Minuit of the Dutch West India Company arranged for the purchase of Manhattan from the Native American population. When the Dutch settlers arrived by boat—many traveling down the Hudson from Fort Orange—their establishment of New Amsterdam was dependent upon water transportation. The initial population of a handful of families grew to a small village of thirty or so houses within the first year, and by 1628, there was an estimated population of about 270 people. By the 1630s, the Dutch began exploring what would become the city's boroughs. Growth continued as more and more immigrants arrived. The newcomers settled first on the opposite shore of the lower East River, where the settlement of Breuckelen would eventually lend its name to the entire area now known as Brooklyn. In 1639, a Swedish captain named Jonas Bronck acquired a large tract of land north of the Harlem River, which was later renamed the Bronx in his honor. Settlers crossed the

9

upper regions of the East River into the outlying area and worked to establish small hamlets, including one known as Flushing (1645) after the port city of Vlissingen in the Netherlands. Attempts were made to populate Staten Island, but the establishment of a permanent settlement did not occur until 1661 due to conflicts with the native population.

New Amsterdam was cosmopolitan from its beginning, as the Dutch were open to living alongside the French, German, English, and any others who ventured into their settlements. By the colony's second generation, multiple languages and religions flourished side by side. Although the seventeenth century was marked by political strife and the Dutch would lose control of their island to the English in 1664, expansion continued and the colony prospered.

As long as a settler had access to water transport, living on the island was not all that difficult. By 1659, Dutch settlers established a ferry service connecting Manhattan and Brooklyn. A second operated between Manhattan and the Bronx beginning in the 1660s. But in order to develop a thriving community, an alternate means of crossing the rivers was necessary—one that wasn't subject to the problems of ice and fog. Bridges were the solution.

Manhattan's first known bridge was a private venture. Under the sponsorship of Dutch merchant and landowner Frederick Philipse, a stone and timber bridge was constructed over the Spuyten Duyvil Creek—a narrow tidal strait that connects the Hudson and Harlem Rivers. Low tides at the meeting point of the creek and the Harlem River made crossing the water relatively easy, and a small enclave known as Fordham (Saxon for "houses by the ford, or wading place") grew up on the Bronx side. It was here that Philipse chose to build his bridge, which opened for use in 1693 near the spot where West 230th Street and Kingsbridge Avenue now intersect in the Bronx.

The Philipse family was adept at land management, shipping, and entrepreneurship in general. Frederick Philipse and his son Adolphe amassed large holdings along the Hudson River and, through strategic ventures in international shipping as well as astute political maneuvering (they swore allegiance to the English in 1664 rather than lose their properties), expanded their wealth. For more than half a century, their drawbridge was the only "land" link between Manhattan and the Bronx. They operated it as a toll bridge and fenced off the shoals of the creek so that the public had no choice but to use it. Everyone was required to pay, with the exception of soldiers and those in the king's service—a situation that caused the crossing to be named the King's Bridge. For the average farmer, this meant an annual fee of 6 to 15 pounds sterling (an estimated $200 to $500 in today's currency) to bring produce and livestock to market. This was a substantial economic burden for a small landholder, and as a result, the Philipse family was deeply resented.

Just like their counterparts today, New Yorkers of the time did not suffer quietly. In 1758, Benjamin Palmer, a merchant and later founder of City Island, publicly declared his intent to establish an alternative bridge between Manhattan and the Bronx. Urging his fellow citizens to support him in the fight against the Philipse family, Palmer constructed a crude stone and timber drawbridge that was nearly two feet (0.6m) wider than the King's Bridge. The new crossing—appropriately known as the Farmer's Free Bridge—stood at what is now West 225th Street and Broadway in the Bronx. In 1776, the British destroyed the structure, but it was quickly rebuilt after the war, performing its service until 1911, when it was demolished.

Above: Looking up the East River, one can identify the Brooklyn, Manhattan, and Williamsburg Bridges. Photographer Irving Underhill shot this image from Lower Manhattan during the 1930s.

The opening of the Farmer's Free Bridge brought an end to the Philipse family's monopoly, forcing them to give up their toll charges on the King's Bridge. The family's estates were confiscated after the American Revolution, and the bridge came under public jurisdiction.

Although the King's Bridge and the Farmer's Free Bridge provided Manhattan with passageways to the Bronx, both structures were located on the western side of the island. By the mid-1770s, it was clear that a crossing between the island's eastern side and the mainland was sorely needed. In 1774, businessman and landowner Lewis Morris petitioned the New York State Assembly for permission to build a bridge where the Third Avenue Bridge (1898) stands today. His project was delayed by the American Revolution, but in 1790, he once again pleaded his case to build a toll bridge over the Harlem River.

Morris's endeavor was part of a larger scheme to convince George Washington to situate the new federal capital in Morrisania, Morris's family estate in the southwestern area of what would become the Bronx. When Morris learned of Pierre-Charles L'Enfant's plan for the District of Columbia, he lost interest in the bridge proposal, ultimately transferring his rights to John B. Coles. The Coles Bridge—a timber drawbridge three hundred feet (91.5m) long and twenty-four feet (7.5m) wide—was completed by 1797. A stone dam, used to harness the energy of the Harlem River to power the small mills along the riverbank, was incorporated into the structure's foundation. Although the bridge was built to facilitate land travel, a lock system allowed water transport to continue.

The Coles Bridge was a moneymaker. A fee of $37\frac{1}{2}$¢ was charged for the average horse-drawn four-wheel carriage. The pedestrian fee was 3¢ per person, and a penny was charged for each ox, cow, or steer. Located near the current intersection of East 130th Street and Third Avenue in Manhattan and crossing over to where Third Avenue resumes in the Bronx, the Coles Bridge diverted eastern travel away from its western counterparts and quickly became the principal artery for people traveling from Manhattan to Connecticut and Boston. The bridge's owners incorporated in 1808, calling themselves the Harlem Bridge Company. In 1858, they tried to extend their charter, but the New York State Assembly refused, turning the bridge's management over instead to the Harlem Bridge Commission, a state-appointed group of public officials from New York and Westchester Counties. The commission oversaw repairs to the Coles Bridge but in 1859 recommended that a new bridge be constructed, as doing so would be easier than having to constantly fix the existing structure. The replacement span was the city's first iron bridge. Situated slightly north of the old bridge, it opened to traffic in 1868.

This second structure—now called the Third Avenue Bridge—also suffered from maintenance issues. Increasing vehicular traffic—including the first railroad service over the Harlem River—combined with the bridge's own weight created stress cracks. Although the structure continued in service through the 1880s, it was determined

that a new bridge was required. In 1892, the New York State Legislature authorized construction of the new crossing, also called the Third Avenue Bridge. Designed by Thomas C. Clarke, the swing bridge was built at a cost of $4 million (more than double the original state appropriation of $1.5 million) and opened to traffic on August 1, 1898. This bridge still stands today.

Within two centuries of settlement, New York had created the beginnings of a public bridge system that would help lead to the city's incorporation. The next century in bridge design would belong to the dreamers who envisioned creating a metropolis linked by the fruits of the new industrial age.

Above: Providing access to the Bronx from the eastern side of Manhattan, the Coles Bridge was a highly successful venture.

Right: Shown here in the late nineteenth century, the King's Bridge—originally completed in 1693 and then rebuilt around 1713—would be a part of the city landscape until 1917. Terminating in the western portion of the Bronx near the present-day intersection of West 230th Street and Kingsbridge Avenue, the structure lent its name to the neighborhood of Kingsbridge. The area was dominated by farming until the early 1860s, when the Johnson Iron Foundry was built to supply weapons to the Union Army. The introduction of the subway to the neighborhood in 1908 led to the area's rapid settlement and urbanization. As technology progressed, the King's Bridge became outdated. Changes in transportation led to the demolition of the structure, as it was feared that the old bridge would not be able to withstand automobile traffic.

Left: The Farmer's Free Bridge was the second bridge built in New York City. Constructed around 1758, it provided people traveling between Manhattan and the Bronx with an alternative to the toll bridge maintained by the Philipse family. Both this bridge and the King's Bridge featured a draw system, allowing boats to travel on the Spuyten Duyvil Creek connecting the Harlem and Hudson Rivers.

Right: This photograph of the Third Avenue Bridge (1868)—New York City's first iron bridge—was taken sometime in the 1890s prior to its demolition. The structure, which was built as a replacement for the Coles Bridge, was itself later replaced by a larger swing bridge that opened to traffic on August 1, 1898.

Left: Pictured here in 1909 is the swing bridge that replaced the Third Avenue Bridge of 1868. Also known as the Third Avenue Bridge (1898), the crossing is still in use today. In fact, traffic on this bridge is so heavy—an estimated 70,000 vehicles per day—that plans commenced in 2001 to rebuild the structure.

Right: The oldest standing bridge in New York City is the High Bridge (1848). Constructed as part of the massive Croton Aqueduct system, the Roman-looking bridge was designed for the purpose of carrying water pipes across the Harlem River. This photograph was taken prior to the construction of the Washington Bridge, which would become the High Bridge's neighbor in the late 1880s.

Below: New York City's bridges have served as the backdrop for many historic events. On July 14, 1938, a twin-propeller Lockheed 14 Super Electra flew over downtown Manhattan and the Brooklyn Bridge (1883). Inside were American millionaire Howard Hughes and his crew, who set a new aviation record by flying around the world in four days.

Above: The Brooklyn Bridge has inspired poets and artists for more than a century. Nighttime views such as this twentieth-century photograph serve as a reminder of the structure's exquisite beauty.

Above: William England, photographer for the London Stereoptic Company, shot this image in 1859. It is one of the earliest photographs of the High Bridge (1848), which was built as part of the Croton Aqueduct system to carry water over the Harlem River to Manhattan. Although the water mains inside the bridge were completed in time for the 1842 inauguration of the aqueduct system, the pedestrian walkway was not finished until 1848.

CHAPTER ONE

Engineering Marvels

In 1800, New Yorkers welcomed the new century and all its potential. Expansion was the overall plan for the city, and building up the transportation grid was an important element for future success. Bridges were crucial to this growth. Writing in 1811, Thomas Pope presented this view in his *Treatise on Bridge Architecture*: "Public spirit is alone wanting to make us the greatest nation on earth and there is nothing more essential to the establishment of that greatness than the building of bridges...."

Prior to the establishment of civil engineering as a profession, bridges in New York and elsewhere were organic constructions, crafted through trial-and-error by farmers, carpenters, and shipwrights. Most bridges were simple wooden structures placed atop a timber or stone footing. They were built as needed and situated in spots where the water level and river width made construction possible. These bridges were subject to washouts, and when pushed out of position or swept downstream, they would be hauled back into place by teams of oxen.

The founding of engineering schools and professional training in land surveying, draftsmanship, and metallurgy resulted in bridge designs that conquered the geographic challenges of earlier generations. Perhaps the biggest innovation was the use of iron, and then steel, to span great waterways. No longer did a bridge builder need to look for shallow areas or narrow passages to position a crossing. The wonders of industrial technology meant anything was possible.

The High Bridge is the oldest surviving bridge in New York City. Spanning the Harlem River near West 170th Street in the Bronx and crossing into Manhattan east of Amsterdam Avenue at 175th Street, it was constructed between the years 1839 and 1848. Unlike the situation with the city's previous bridges, the span's main purpose was not to service passenger traffic; rather the structure, which was modeled after classical Roman aqueduct designs, was built as part of the Croton Aqueduct system to carry water to the citizens of Manhattan. John Bloomfield Jervis, chief engineer of the Croton Aqueduct (and former chief engineer of the Erie Canal), was the bridge's creator.

Design and construction of the High Bridge was complicated due to previous access problems with the Harlem River. In 1800, Alexander Macomb had acquired land along the Harlem River with the intent of diverting the waters of the Spuyten Duyvil Creek to power a gristmill. A decade or so later, his son Robert obtained permission from the New York State Legislature to construct a dam and toll bridge across the Harlem River near West 155th Street in

Manhattan. Written into the agreement was the proviso that the waterway remain navigable with the addition of a manned lock—a detail Robert Macomb chose to overlook. At high tide, the dam gates were opened to allow water to flow into the river, as well as to permit limited boat access. The gates were closed as soon as the tide changed so that the ebbing waters could be harnessed to power the gristmill and other small industries. Unlike the earlier Harlem River bridges that featured a drawbridge style of construction, the Macombs Dam Bridge (1814) was stationary and thereby prevented through traffic on the river.

Public frustration over the lack of access grew, and the courts were petitioned for redress. Finally, a group of citizens took matters into their own hands. In 1838, led by Lewis G. Morris (son of the original owner of the Coles Bridge patent), they chartered a ship for the stated purpose of delivering coal up the Harlem River. Upon reaching the dam, they demanded passage, knowing that no locks were available. When, of course, no means of passage was provided, they broke through the Macombs Dam Bridge. The incident led to a trial, and the courts ruled against the Renwick family (who had purchased the dam from Robert Macomb), finding in favor of Morris and his friends. As a result, it was determined that there existed in New York, as well as in the entire United States, the right to navigable passage on tidal waterways, a ruling that would impact all future bridge building in New York City. (The original Macombs Dam Bridge would have two subsequent replacements, the latter of which was completed in 1895 and still stands today.)

Indeed, the Macombs Dam Bridge case had an effect upon the design of the High Bridge. John Jervis originally proposed a low-profile drawbridge that would be in keeping with the landscape and visually unobtrusive—an approach supported by the New York Water Commission. Opponents, however, argued for a grand design of mammoth proportions that would cut across the valley at a continuous high grade. Both camps used the newspapers to advocate their preferred designs. But, using the problems with the original Macombs Dam Bridge to bolster their case, Jervis's opponents argued that his drawbridge design could not possibly provide the width and height clearances required for safe passage on the river.

The New York State Legislature settled the debate by mandating either that the proposed aqueduct be both high and wide enough for ships to pass freely underneath (at least eighty feet [24.5m] across at high tide) or, conversely, that the pipes be buried beneath the riverbed. Jervis analyzed both approaches and reluctantly concluded that because they did not have enough experience with tunneling and excavation, it would probably be more cost-efficient to go with the higher (and more elaborate) bridge design.

The New York Water Commission appropriated $950,000 for construction of a 1,450-foot (442m)-long granite viaduct that would stretch across the Harlem River Valley. Jervis's revised design incorporated fifteen arches, eight of which were situated in the water providing a series of 80-feet (24.5m)-wide passages for boats. Also proposing a high-tide height of 114 feet (35m) above the river's surface, the new plans satisfied everyone that the High Bridge would provide more than enough room for a ship to pass without damage. Within the walls, two water pipes—each thirty-three inches (84cm) in diameter—were laid; years later, the addition of a third pipe was required to handle the growing city's water requirements. Despite Jervis's initial reluctance, the High Bridge was considered a masterpiece and quickly became a tourist attraction. Its opening was celebrated on July 4, 1842, even though the pedestrian walkway was still a few years from completion. A forty-one-gun salute was given—one for each mile of the aqueduct—and water was released into the Murray Hill distribution reservoir (the current site of the New York Public Library) for the first time.

Dreams of monumental bridges were not limited to the citizens of northern Manhattan and the Bronx. For centuries, transportation from Manhattan to Brooklyn and Queens was limited to ferry service and, hence, subject to the whims of nature. Throughout the eighteenth century and into the nineteenth, ideas were discussed and plans formulated for creating a crossing over the East River. But prior to the Industrial Revolution, building techniques prohibited such an undertaking. Hope came with the introduction of iron into bridge making; Harlem River bridge makers took the lead by replacing the timber and stone Coles Bridge with the city's first iron bridge in 1868. It was not until the widespread use of steel took hold that an East River crossing would become a reality.

John Augustus Roebling was the person who would conquer the East River. A German immigrant, he possessed a civil engineering degree and had had modest success as a bridge and road builder by the time he came to the United States in 1831. On American shores, he gained confidence and experience working on projects such as the Niagara Suspension Bridge (1855)—the world's first successful railroad suspension bridge—and the Cincinnati–Covington Bridge (1866), which spans the Ohio River from Cincinnati, Ohio, to Covington, Kentucky. All was rehearsal for his masterpiece: the Brooklyn Bridge, an idea he had been considering since 1852, as he worked on the Niagara project. In 1867, Roebling presented his concept to the New York Bridge Company: "The contemplated work, when constructed in accordance with my design, will not only be the greatest bridge in existence, but it will be the greatest engineering work on this continent, and of the age."

There was no question that by the middle of the nineteenth century an East River bridge was needed. Brooklyn was booming with new construction as more and more area residents chose to work on one shore and live on the other. In April 1867, the New York State Legislature approved plans "to incorporate the New York Bridge Company for the purpose of constructing and maintaining a bridge across the East River." The funding package was divided between Manhattan and Brooklyn, with the former responsible for

Right: John Augustus Roebling came to the United States in 1831. Despite his previous engineering education and experience, he began his American life as a farmer before obtaining employment as a civil engineer with the Sandy and Beaver Canal Company. Roebling developed a sturdy wire cable, which he felt was a better alternative to hemp rope in industrial use. He tested his product on a series of suspension aqueducts and established a wire cable factory in Trenton, New Jersey. Roebling's first wire cable suspension bridges were the Niagara Suspension Bridge and the Cincinnati–Covington Bridge.

one-third of the cost and the latter shouldering the rest. Roebling was hired as chief engineer at an annual salary of $8,000, and the design process commenced. His experience with suspension projects and his understanding of the limits of technology and available materials allowed him to turn around a concept within three months. He was convinced that any span of less than 3,000 feet (914.5m) was feasible and explained to his bosses that "a span of 1,600 feet [487.5m] or more can be made virtually as safe and as strong in proportion to a span of 100 feet [30.5m]." Roebling proposed the construction of two massive anchors—one on each side of the river—and a system of iron trusses and steel cables. Traffic lanes would exist for pedestrians, vehicles, and trains. And a toll system would allow the bridge to pay for itself, especially if the numbers reached his estimate of forty million people per year. The redesign and approval process went on for about two years. In June 1869, Roebling received the go-ahead to proceed with the project. Unfortunately, he was injured in a dock accident when an incoming ferry crushed his foot; he died of complications three weeks later. His son, Colonel Washington Augustus Roebling, was tapped as his replacement.

Colonel Washington Roebling came to the project with an engineering degree from Rensselaer Polytechnic Institute in upstate New York and a background of practical experience building bridges for the Union Army during the Civil War. In preparation for assisting his father with the Brooklyn Bridge, he had also traveled through Europe to study the use of new materials, such as steel, and the implementation of new techniques, such as the building of caisson foundations. Although only thirty-two years old, Washington Roebling was ready to step in and take over the project.

It would take more than five years to build the anchors and structural towers for the Brooklyn Bridge. Pneumatic caissons were required for conducting the underwater excavation on both sides of the river. On the Brooklyn side, the workers dug below the riverbed into the bedrock to create a solid foundation. Due to massive boulders and other obstructions, work proceeded slowly; there were some days when only six inches (15cm) of progress were made. Eighteen months after commencement, the workers reached ninety feet (27.5m), and work on the Brooklyn side was declared to be complete. Work on the Manhattan side, however, was much more difficult as the workers struggled through a combination of bedrock, quicksand, and gravel. After another three years, Roebling declared that the Manhattan foundation could rest at seventy feet (21.5m)—not as deep as he would have liked, but secure nonetheless.

Workers in the pneumatic caissons were subject to horrific conditions. Blowouts would occur when compressed air rushed out of the chamber, only to be replaced by water and debris. These events were more frightening than dangerous. More threatening was the potential for a fire, as the caissons were made of wood and lit by gas lamps. A major fire did occur in 1870 on the Brooklyn side; the caisson had to be flooded in order to put the inferno out, and then the chamber had to be refitted so that work could resume. The greatest danger, though, was a medical condition referred to as caisson disease or "the bends." At the time, much was unknown about the effects of working underwater at high pressures. Years later the problem was identified as the release of nitrogen bubbles in muscle tissue. If a worker reached the surface too quickly without proper decompression, he could be subject to cramping, paralysis, or even death. During construction on the Brooklyn side, only six men were diagnosed with caisson disease. But on the Manhattan side, there were more than one hundred cases, including Washington Roebling himself. In 1872, Roebling became so debilitated by the condition that he was unable to work. He finally recovered to

Right: The public's interest in the Brooklyn Bridge was strong, and the project's progress was well documented from the start. *Frank Leslie's Illustrated Newspaper* was one of the first to publish stories on the construction process, producing full-page story sheets explaining the various engineering techniques employed. The work involving the pneumatic caissons was especially fascinating to most people, as this was one of the first times that this method of bridge construction was used.

such a point that he was able to direct progress on the bridge—from his bed. For the next ten years, his wife, Emily Warren Roebling, was his eyes, ears, and voice on the project; she became the de facto supervisor of the Brooklyn Bridge's construction.

Work continued on the bridge. Upon completion of the towers and anchorage system, the next task was the stringing of steel cable with a tested strength of 160,000 pounds (72,640kg) per inch (2.5cm). There were problems with defective materials from the suppliers, but on October 5, 1878, the last wire was in place. By this time, the project had reached its budgetary limits and charges of corruption were being thrown about. In November 1878, work on the bridge was suspended due to a lack of funds, but the New York State Legislature eventually came through with more money and the project resumed. The Brooklyn Bridge was completed in the spring of 1883, and the grand opening was held on May 24 of that year. Complete with parades, speeches, and fireworks, the ceremonies were spectacular. President Chester A. Arthur was in attendance, as were the mayors of Brooklyn and New York (Brooklyn was its own city at the time). Missing, however, was Washington Roebling, whose poor health prevented him from participating in the celebratory event.

Left: Colonel Washington Augustus Roebling is illustrated viewing the Brooklyn Bridge from his home in Brooklyn Heights. A hands-on civil engineer, Roebling toiled side by side with his workers until he fell victim to the debilitating caisson disease.

Above: The High Bridge was originally built with fifteen arches, eight of which were situated over the Harlem River. As a result of early-nineteenth-century restrictions imposed to allow for boat traffic, those eight water-spanning arches were each 80 feet (24.5m) wide at the high-tide mark, thereby providing more than enough space for the passage of steamboats such as this one circa 1895. However, by the early twentieth century, the U.S. Army Corps of Engineers determined that the bridge's water spans were too narrow for modern vessels and retrofitting was required. In 1927, it was decided that four river piers and five arches be removed and replaced with a single steel arch providing a 360-foot (110m)-wide clearance.

Right: Modeled after a Roman aqueduct, the High Bridge is considered the first of New York City's great bridges. The 1,450-foot (442m)-long granite viaduct, which stretches across the Harlem River Valley, cost approximately $963,000 to construct. Initially, the bridge contained two mains, each 33 inches (84cm) in diameter, to carry water from the Croton Dam to New York City—a distance of 41 miles (66km). This photograph was taken circa 1895.

Above: From its opening, the pedestrian walkway on the High Bridge was a visitor attraction. Taking a stroll on the bridge, after all, was a pleasant way to spend an afternoon. The walkway was closed in the 1970s after numerous instances of people using it as a point from which to drop large pieces of stone and other items on boats passing beneath the bridge. The renovation and rededication of Highbridge Park in early 2002 initiated public discussion about reopening the High Bridge to pedestrian traffic.

Right: Looking north, one can spy the Washington Bridge (1888) through the stone arches of the High Bridge in this circa 1910 photograph of the Harlem River Speedway, an exercise area and race-track completed in 1898. Horse racing was always popular in New York City and the surrounding areas, and has been traced back as far as 1665, when the Newmarket Track was opened at Salisbury Plain (present-day Hempstead, Long Island).

Above: Three riders head north on the Harlem River Speedway toward the High and Washington Bridges. The ninety-five-foot (29m)-wide roadway along the Harlem River in Manhattan stretched two miles (3.2km) from West 155th Street to West 208th Street and was flanked by greenery and pedestrian walkways. The speedway was later paved over to become part of the Harlem River Drive.

Right: Security concerns resulted in the closing of the High Bridge water mains in 1917. The United States was on the verge of war with Germany, and it was feared that attempts would be made to flood the city by bombing the aqueduct. Focus was placed on protecting the New Croton Aqueduct (1890) and the Catskill Reservoir (1926), which was under construction at the time.

Opposite, top: New Yorkers view the opening of the Harlem River Ship Canal, which facilitated travel around the northern portion of Manhattan. Work on the project began in 1826, and on June 17, 1895, the first portion opened to traffic. The canal cut through rock outcroppings between Inwood and Marble Hill in northern Manhattan, making Marble Hill part of the Bronx upon the canal's completion in 1938. In the background of the photograph is the third Macombs Dam Bridge (1895), a Gothic Revival–style steel swing bridge located at 155th Street and 7th Avenue in Manhattan and connecting to Jerome Avenue at 161st Street in the Bronx. Designed by Alfred Pancoast Boller, the 408-foot (123.5m) span, which cost $1.36 million, was the third bridge on the site originally occupied by the first Macombs Dam Bridge (1814). The second bridge, known as the Central Bridge (1861), was an iron and wood structure constructed for the more modest sum of $50,000.

Opposite: It took a total of five years to build the two towers of the Brooklyn Bridge. This 1872 photograph by S.A. Holmes shows the nearly completed tower on the Brooklyn side. Progressing at an average of twelve to eighteen inches (30–46cm) per day, the pneumatic caisson for this tower was slowly sunk to its final destination of ninety feet (27.5m) below the riverbed, reaching this spot after more than a year and a half of work. Construction of the Manhattan tower was more difficult, as excavation workers encountered solid rock on top of quicksand, which in turn had cemented gravel underneath it. As a result, the Manhattan tower foundation— which took twice as long to complete as the Brooklyn tower foundation—rests at seventy feet (21.5m) below the riverbed.

Above: By 1875, the time of this photograph, the Brooklyn and Manhattan towers and their anchorages were in the final stage of construction. More than five years had passed since work began on the Brooklyn Bridge, and it would take another eight years before it would be finished.

Above: This 1876 panoramic view shows the western tower of the Brooklyn Bridge rising against the landscape of Lower Manhattan. In the distance is the Hudson River, which would be the great challenge of twentieth-century bridge engineers.

Below: The completed Brooklyn and Manhattan towers are featured in this image. In the foreground, work continues on one of the anchorage structures, which were designed to provide tension on the suspension cables and give additional support to the towers; this extra support was created to prevent the pressure of the vertical load of the bridge deck span from causing the towers to bend inward. Each anchorage was constructed with an estimated sixty thousand tons (54,420t) of granite and incorporated four iron anchor plates in its base—one for each of the suspension cables.

Right: It was not until the late nineteenth century that newspapers were able to print actual photographs. As a result, publications depended on skilled engravers to translate photographs to the printed page. This engraving from *Harper's New Monthly Magazine* illustrates workers splicing steel wire on the drums during the construction of the Brooklyn Bridge. The first cable was strung from anchorage to anchorage on August 14, 1876. This "traveler" rope was then incorporated into a pulley system for hauling larger cables and supplies across the East River. On August 25, the bridge's master mechanic, E.F. Farrington, climbed into a sling chair suspended on the traveler rope and was pulled across the river. Twenty-two minutes later, he landed on the Manhattan side and had the honor of being the first person to cross the "bridge."

Opposite: Workers prepare the steel wire bundles that will form one of the four cables supporting the Brooklyn Bridge. Each of the cables is composed of 19 individual wire bundles, or strands, which in turn contain 286 individual wires that have the thickness of a lead pencil. A single cable contains approximately 3,515 miles (5,656km) of wire—more than the distance between the Atlantic and Pacific shores of the United States.

Right, top: This engraving from *Harper's New Monthly Magazine* shows the process of cable spinning, in which workers wrapped wire around the entire length of the cable to create a solid steel beam. This stage of construction would be completed in October 1878.

Right, bottom: Engineers pose on the cable spinning platform circa 1878. In the foreground are sections of the steel truss deck, which would be installed upon completion of the cables.

Above: Brooklyn Bridge engineers and local dignitaries inspect the cable spinning process.

Above: Photographer S.A. Holmes recorded the construction of the Brooklyn Bridge approaches on both sides of the East River. Underneath these ramps, shops and warehouses were built in order to make use of the space.

Left: Two men study the progress being made on the Brooklyn Bridge from a high catwalk in 1877. In the background is Manhattan, its waterfront filled with ships and ferries. Beneath the men is the unfinished deck, or roadway, being attached to the suspension cables.

The Trustees of the

New York and Brooklyn Bridge

request the honor of the presence of

Edward W. Coit, Esq.

at the

Opening Ceremonies

to take place on Thursday. May twenty fourth, at two o'clock. P. M.

Committees.

On behalf of the Board of Trustees.	William C. Kingsley, Prest. Henry W. Slocum. Jenkins Van Schaick. James S. T. Stranahan. John T. Agnew. Otto Witte.
On behalf of the Cities.	Seth Low, Mayor of Brooklyn. Franklin Edson, Mayor of New York.
On behalf of the Engineers.	Washington A. Roebling.

TIFFANY & CO.

Above: A formal invitation to the opening ceremonies of the Brooklyn Bridge was a social coup, but a lack of one did not prevent people from joining in the celebration. Tens of thousands of people lined both sides of the East River on May 24, 1883, with many able to cross the bridge on its very first day of service.

Opposite, bottom: Opening day featured many hours of festivities. Underneath the Brooklyn Bridge was a flotilla of ships, including the Atlantic Fleet of the U.S. Navy, which boomed out its approval with whistles, bells, and a gun salute. Dignitaries included President Chester A. Arthur and New York governor Grover Cleveland. The evening concluded with a magnificent fireworks display that lasted an entire hour, while a full moon climbed overhead to shine down on what would be called "the eighth wonder of the world." News of the events spread throughout the country, thanks to publications such as *Harper's Weekly*, which carried illustrations such as this one.

Above: People mill about on a roadway approach to the Brooklyn Bridge. Large areas of Brooklyn and Manhattan were cleared in preparation for building the bridge, and while the engineers focused on crossing the river, architects examined how to incorporate the cleared space into the overall look of the project.

Opposite: Upon its completion, the Brooklyn Bridge was the first steel-wire suspension bridge in the world. At nearly 1,600 feet (488m) long (almost 6,000 feet [1,829m] if the approach ramps are included), the structure also carried the title of world's longest bridge until 1889, when the Firth of Forth—a cantilever bridge in Scotland—captured the title.

Right: Following the fireworks celebration on opening day in 1883, the promenade of the Brooklyn Bridge was lit with electrical lights for the first time. The United States Electric Lighting Company— a pioneer in the illumination of New York City—had received one of the city's first franchises on May 3, 1881, for the right to serve Manhattan south of 136th Street. Although the Edison Electric Illuminating Company opened the first substation on September 4, 1882, the United States Electric Lighting Company had its own coup with the capture of the Brooklyn Bridge contract—an accomplishment they touted on this 1899 advertising card.

Left: A stroll on the Brooklyn Bridge was a popular pastime, offering magnificent views up and down the East River, as well as of each shore.

Below: By the time of this early-twentieth-century image, the Brooklyn Bridge was an established part of the New York City landscape.

Opposite: William J. Gaynor served as mayor of New York City from 1909 to 1913. During his four years in office, Mayor Gaynor commuted to City Hall via the Brooklyn Bridge. The Democrat's reform policies did not endear him to the powers at Tammany Hall, who blocked his renomination on the party ticket. He announced his intent to run for reelection as an Independent candidate, but he died while traveling to England on September 12, 1913—possibly from lingering health problems caused by a 1910 assassination attempt.

Above: Carriage traffic on the Brooklyn Bridge, shown here around 1915, would be surpassed in the 1920s by the automobile. Upon the bridge's opening, the center area was reserved for pedestrians, while the inside traffic lanes catered to railroad cars and the outside lanes served horse-drawn vehicles. Today, pedestrians still use the center promenade, but all vehicle lanes are devoted to automobile traffic.

Opposite, top: In the 1930s, photographer Berenice Abbott began a documentary project about New York City. She sought to capture all five boroughs, and in 1939, the collection was published as *Changing New York*. Today it is considered one of the best visual records of the city prior to World War II. This 1937 photograph of the Brooklyn Bridge includes a view of Pier 21, used by the Pennsylvania Railroad and the Baltimore and Ohio Railroad. The image emphasizes the continued industrial vitality found underneath the approaches to the bridge.

Opposite, bottom: American actors Jules Munshin, Frank Sinatra, and Gene Kelly (left to right) stand on the Brooklyn Bridge in this movie still from Stanley Donen and Gene Kelly's 1949 film *On the Town*.

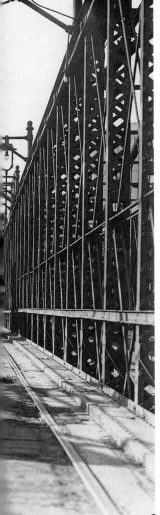

Above: Photographer William Henry Jackson documented the Washington Bridge in 1890, not long after its opening. Jackson was an early photographer of the American West. In 1869, he photographed construction of the Union Pacific Railroad, and his images of Yellowstone contributed to Congress's decision to declare it the first national park in 1872. Jackson was one of the best-known photographers in the Detroit Publishing Company, the original distributor of this image.

CHAPTER TWO

A City Joined

Bridge building continued at a fast clip for the remainder of the nineteenth century, with an additional Harlem River crossing between Manhattan and the Bronx capturing much attention. In 1888, the Washington Bridge connected West 181st Street in Manhattan and University Avenue in the Bronx. This steel arched bridge was referred to as the Harlem River Bridge and the Manhattan Bridge in its early days, but its name was changed in 1889 to commemorate the centennial of George Washington's inauguration as the country's first president. Designed by Charles C. Schneider and Wilhelm Hildenbrand, it is the third oldest standing bridge in New York City. The Washington Bridge was an exercise in efficiency, completed for pedestrian traffic in only two years. Upon the bridge's opening, *The New York Times* hailed the accomplishment as a "marvel of rapidity of construction." The newspaper went on to describe the bridge as "one of the most imposing, beautiful, and substantial to be found in any metropolis...."

Bridge design was important to New Yorkers, who debated issues of aesthetics as hotly as concerns regarding safety and construction. Indeed, this was the case with the Williamsburg Bridge. Built in response to the high demand for additional East River crossings, which increased as the boroughs east of Manhattan developed rapidly, this utilitarian structure suffered from a tremendous amount of public criticism. Located upriver from the Brooklyn Bridge, it evoked a much different public response than that of its graceful neighbor.

Completed in 1903, the Williamsburg Bridge was built over the course of seven years—half the time spent on the Brooklyn Bridge. The *Brooklyn Daily Times* tried to inspire pride in its review of the bridge by stressing, "The aim of the Greeks in their works was beauty. The object wrought in our time is of utility, and the Williamsburg Bridge is the very temple, the highest achievement of the utilitarian." Most other commentaries were not so diplomatic. In October 1905, critic Montgomery Schuyler went so far as to flat out condemn the finished product in *Architectural Record*: "...the designer has done his worst to make his bridge look ugly....Outside of what had to be right about the Williamsburg Bridge, it may be said that everything is wrong."

Leffert L. Buck was the unfortunate designer of the Williamsburg Bridge. Possessing a mechanical approach to engineering, he focused on the ability of the materials to carry out their purpose rather than on trying to achieve a marriage of beauty and strength. Buck was

Above: The Washington Bridge is the third oldest standing bridge in New York City. Charles C. Schneider, who won the design contest sponsored by the city, developed the span in conjunction with Wilhelm Hildenbrand. The duo's original plan came with a construction estimate of $3 million, but they were requested to come up with a more modestly priced design. In response, Schneider substituted steel for ornamental ironwork, but it was the ingenious use of plate girders on the arch ribs that lent the Washington Bridge a certain grace reminiscent of European bridges.

a graduate of Rensselaer Polytechnic Institute and had begun his career working for a fellow alumnus, Washington Roebling. The Williamsburg Bridge was to be Buck's masterpiece, but he lacked the artistic sensibilities of both his mentor Roebling and his future boss Gustav Lindenthal. What's more, the design plans for the Williamsburg Bridge—unlike those for later projects—were not subject to a unified city review. There was grumbling during the design process that the look of the bridge was not quite up to New York's standards, but there was no one to address the problem from a position of public authority. With the incorporation of the five boroughs into the City of New York in 1898—a year after Buck's final design was approved and put into construction—a new bridge commission possessing the power to oversee municipal engineering projects was formed. In 1902, newly elected mayor Seth Low appointed Gustav Lindenthal as New York City's bridge commissioner.

A firm believer in the melding of aesthetic design and engineering, Lindenthal tried to salvage the look of the Williamsburg Bridge. Toward that end, he "promoted" Buck from chief engineer of the project to overall consulting engineer for the bridge commission and brought aboard architect Henry Hornbostel. However, by the time Lindenthal and Hornbostel got involved, it was simply too late. (The pair would later have much success collaborating on two of the city's greatest river crossing projects: the Queensboro Bridge and the Hell

Gate Bridge.) Lindenthal made the best of the situation in his dedication speech by speaking of future greatness. After stressing the significance of the Williamsburg Bridge as the first bridge constructed by the incorporated City of New York, he proclaimed, "Our city will be preeminently the city of great bridges, representing emphatically for centuries to come the civilization of our age, the age of iron and steel."

During his two years as commissioner of the New York City Department of Bridges, Gustav Lindenthal would emphasize the interdependence of aesthetic design and physical construction. In addition to his attempts to rehabilitate the Williamsburg Bridge, Lindenthal oversaw repairs and restoration of the Brooklyn Bridge. But the most important contributions during his appointment were the design of the Queensboro Bridge and the preparation of the original plans for the Manhattan Bridge.

The Queensboro Bridge would become the third East River crossing upon its completion in March 1909. Unlike its predecessors, this span is not a suspension bridge, but rather a cantilever bridge. The two-level steel structure connects Manhattan's East 59th Street with Long Island City in Queens and is often referred to as the 59th Street Bridge. The idea for this crossing originated in designs from the 1860s, when the future bridge was known as Blackwell's Island Bridge. An accepted design existed and was under construction when Lindenthal took over as bridge commissioner in 1902, but after his experiences with the Williamsburg Bridge design controversy, he scrapped the plans and reworked the project in collaboration with architect Henry Hornbostel. Their design was submitted for approval in 1903, and work on the new bridge commenced.

The Queensboro Bridge, like many of the city's other engineering projects, had its share of problems. In 1904, Mayor Seth Low lost his reelection campaign to George McClellan, who promptly replaced Lindenthal with George E. Best as bridge commissioner. Along with the change in leadership, the Queensboro project was plagued by such delays as wind damage, union sabotage, and a steelworkers' strike. What's more, five years into the project, a similar cantilever design failed in Quebec, prompting safety concerns regarding the Queensboro Bridge's structural soundness and questions about its potential for weight overload. An independent engineering survey was conducted, and the results led Lindenthal—who had remained on the project as designer—to lighten the load on the Queensboro Bridge by reducing the number of planned elevated railroad tracks from four to two. Finished in 1909, the Queensboro Bridge was acknowledged as Lindenthal's success, proof that good engineering and an attractive design could coexist. With this triumph, Lindenthal redeemed New York's reputation as a city of great bridges.

At the same time that the Queensboro Bridge was being constructed, a fourth East River crossing was under way. This project began under Lindenthal's watch as bridge commissioner, but was

Above: The first plans for a cantilever span at the site of the Queensboro Bridge were presented by C.A. Trowbridge in 1868. But it was not until 1899 that funding was appropriated for the project, at which point a second design was submitted by R.S. Buck. Although Buck's design was accepted and approved by the U.S. Army Corps of Engineers in 1901, Gustav Lindenthal chose to rework the entire project when he became the city's bridge commissioner in 1902.

completely revised upon his departure in 1904. Located between the Brooklyn and Williamsburg Bridges, the Manhattan Bridge was originally planned as a suspension span using a relatively new process of eyebar chain construction rather than cable wire. But in New York City, then as now, politics was everything, and the new bridge commissioner, George Best, scrapped Lindenthal's 1903 design. Unlike the Queensboro Bridge, which was under construction upon Best's arrival, the Manhattan Bridge was still on the drawing board, and Best seized the opportunity to make his mark on New York's landscape. He hired Leon S. Moisseiff to redesign the bridge. The new version did incorporate some of Lindenthal's ideas, namely flexible two-dimensional towers that would expand and contract along with the suspension cables. But instead of going along with the eyebar chain proposal, Moisseiff reverted to the traditional approach of utilizing steel cable wire for construction. He applied a relatively new concept known as the "deflection theory." Developed by Austrian engineer Josef Melan, the deflection theory examined the interaction of opposing forces. Moisseiff's application centered on the idea that the downward force caused by the weight of the bridge deck, or roadway, would be counterbalanced by an upward force pulling both left and right by the tension on the suspension cables.

Lindenthal denounced the redesign, airing his arguments publicly in the newspapers. Indeed, Moisseiff did not adequately respond to Lindenthal's concern that the redesign could not support the planned weight load of two roadways, four trolley lines, and four elevated railroad tracks. A major source of uncertainty was what would occur when the subway trains were on the bridge. Unlike the Williamsburg Bridge, where the tracks run along the inside lanes, the Manhattan Bridge features tracks along the outside lanes. As a result, when subway trains running in opposite directions simultaneously begin their crossing, the Manhattan Bridge twists up to four feet (1m) in opposing directions. The vibrations caused by this design have led to numerous retrofits and strengthening measures over the years.

Despite the problems that resulted from Moisseiff's first application of the deflection theory, his development of its principles with respect to suspension bridges would prove invaluable to future engineers by allowing for the design of longer spans. The Manhattan Bridge opened on December 31, 1909, in time to meet the deadline set by McClellan, who wanted its dedication to be his last official act as mayor.

Gustav Lindenthal returned to railroad bridge design in the years following his work for the bridge commission. He consulted on a project to connect the Pennsylvania Railroad (which included the Long Island Rail Road) with the New York, New Haven and Hartford Railroad line in order to facilitate passage to and from points east and west of Manhattan.

In 1910, the Pennsylvania Railroad had just completed construction of its tunnel service connecting New Jersey with Manhattan, marking an end to forced ferry transport across the Hudson River for both passengers and freight alike. Lindenthal's task was to provide a solution for trains traveling between New York City and New England or Long Island that faced the problem of crossing the Harlem and East Rivers.

To meet this demand, Lindenthal designed a 3.2-mile (5km) system of bridges, viaducts, and overpasses running through Queens, across Wards Island, and into the Bronx to connect with Manhattan. The centerpiece of the project was the New York Connecting Bridge, commonly called the Hell Gate Bridge (1916). With its 1,017-foot (310m) steel arch, the Hell Gate Bridge set a record, becoming not only the longest steel arch bridge in the world, but also the first with a span of more than 1,000 feet (305m). Othmar H. Ammann, Lindenthal's chief assistant, described the bridge as a "monumental portal for the steamers which enter New York Harbor from Long Island Sound" and praised his boss's understanding of the importance of the span's design, as the structure would be highly visible from many points in the city. Ammann learned his lessons well from Lindenthal and became New York's master bridge builder of the twentieth century. Accomplishing something his mentor could not, Ammann successfully conquered the city's final challenge: spanning the Hudson River.

Above: Gustav Lindenthal was one of New York City's premier bridge designers and engineers. Under his watch as the city's first bridge commissioner, a number of projects were undertaken, including the design and construction of the Queensboro Bridge.

Below: Photographer Berenice Abbott made a number of visits to the Manhattan Bridge as part of her documentary project on the changing New York landscape. This image, taken from Pike and Henry Streets in Brooklyn, was shot on March 6, 1936.

Right: Norman Wurts photographed the Washington Bridge (1888) as it neared completion. Crossing the Harlem River, the span connects Manhattan's West 181st Street with University Avenue in the Bronx. This steel and iron structure was the first New York City bridge to incorporate plate girders in its arch design, giving it the look of masonry while allowing the project to remain on budget.

Left: The Washington Bridge was designed to accommodate both pedestrian and vehicular traffic. On December 1, 1888, its two fifteen-foot (4.5m)-wide walkways opened to the public—ahead of the rest of the bridge, which wasn't yet ready. Although the entire bridge was supposed to open on February 22, 1889— George Washington's birthday—conflict within the city government kept it closed to vehicular traffic. Tired of the delay, frustrated citizens removed the barricades in December 1889 to begin full use of the bridge.

Above: Irving Underhill's 1901 overview of the Williamsburg Bridge shows the suspension cables and steel lattice-work, or stiffening trusses, in place. The next stage of construction would be to join the deck span to the hanging supports. The structure was the first suspension bridge to be built with towers made entirely of steel.

Below: Corlear's Hook Park is located just south of the Williamsburg Bridge in Manhattan. At the time of this photograph, the area was the site of dilapidated tenements and waterfront piers (though by the 1950s it would be cleaned up and transformed into a middle-class neighborhood). In the background is the nearly completed bridge, thereby dating this photograph to circa 1901–1902.

Above: A severe fire broke out on November 10, 1902, causing damage to the catwalks and suspension cables of the Williamsburg Bridge. When this photograph was taken—nearly two weeks later on November 22—pieces of the damaged catwalk were still hanging from the cables.

Above: Construction of bridge approaches added almost 6,000 feet (1,829m) to the overall length of the Williamsburg Bridge. Thanks to its main span of 1,600 feet (487.5m)—only 4.5 feet (1.5m) longer than the Brooklyn Bridge—it earned the title of longest (and heaviest) suspension bridge in the world upon its completion.

Below: The Williamsburg Bridge opened for traffic on December 19, 1903. For the first five years, the bridge was the exclusive domain of pedestrians and horse-drawn vehicles. This Bertrand Brown photograph, shot from the pedestrian walkway, shows the tracks built in anticipation of train service, which would be introduced on the span in 1908 by the Brooklyn Elevated System.

Above: The Williamsburg Bridge did not receive the accolades garnered by its East River neighbor, the Brooklyn Bridge (1883). On the contrary, there was hardly a good word said about the bridge or its designer, Leffert L. Buck.

Opposite: Although design critics denounced the Williamsburg Bridge, photographer Berenice Abbott managed to find beauty in its structure when she shot this image on April 28, 1937, as part of her documentary on the changing city. Her location was 6th and Berry Streets on the Brooklyn side of the bridge.

Above: The Williamsburg Bridge helped to strengthen the connection between the boroughs of Manhattan and Brooklyn. In his dedication speech, Mayor Seth Low stated that, thanks to the Brooklyn and Williamsburg Bridges, "the East River has become a highway running through the city instead of a stream dividing two cities from each other."

Left, top: The Queensboro Bridge is nearing completion in this circa 1907 photograph. Designed as the third East River crossing, the span was a masterpiece developed by Gustav Lindenthal, who was determined to regain New York's reputation as a "city of great bridges" in the wake of the criticism evoked by the Williamsburg Bridge. Unlike its predecessors, the Queensboro Bridge featured a cantilever design rather than a suspension system. A traveling crane was used to build the span outward over the water.

Left, bottom: March 30, 1909, marked the opening day of the Queensboro Bridge. Its planners were determined to have a celebration that would rival all others. New York governor Charles Evans Hughes and other dignitaries made speeches, but the high point of the day was a two-hour fireworks extravaganza that included a multicolored representation of Niagara Falls.

Opposite: As with the other East River crossings, the Queensboro Bridge was open to foot traffic. In fact, much of its detailing is best appreciated on foot, as architect Henry Hornbostel included a number of small adornments in his decorative enhancement of Lindenthal's structural design.

Below: Photographer Berenice Abbott included the Queensboro Bridge in her documentation of New York. This image was taken on May 25, 1936, looking southwest from the pier at 41st Road in Queens.

Above: Nighttime brings out the pure design of many of New York's architectural monuments, including the city's bridges. This photograph, taken in 1966, shows the Queensboro Bridge and a good portion of the Manhattan skyline illuminated in all their glory.

Above: The Manhattan Bridge (1909) was the fourth East River crossing to be completed, and it featured a new element in bridge design: two-dimensional tower construction. The purpose of this design strategy—which was included in Gustav Lindenthal's original plans—was to allow the structure to expand and contract as needed.

Left: Workers walk across the catwalk of the Manhattan Bridge pulling suspension cables, which form the spine of the bridge.

Right: This image was shot from the top of the Brooklyn tower of the Manhattan Bridge. Steamships and barges move along the East River, while the Brooklyn Bridge presides grandly over the scene. The wood scaffolding in the foreground is the catwalk.

Below: Workers sit at the top of one of the Manhattan Bridge towers. Note that they're unprotected by modern-day safety nets. In the event of an industrial accident, all that would have stood between them and the East River were suspension cables and fresh air.

Above: Workers atop the catwalk on the Manhattan Bridge attach hanging wire to the primary suspension cables as they prepare to install the bridge's roadway deck. In the distance are the Brooklyn Bridge and the skyline of Lower Manhattan.

Opposite: With the hanging wires and suspension cables in place, work is ready to begin on installation of the roadway deck for the Manhattan Bridge. When finished, the span would be approximately 1,470 feet (448m), slightly shorter than the Brooklyn and Williamsburg Bridges, with lengths of 1,595 feet (486m) and 1,600 feet (487.5m) respectively.

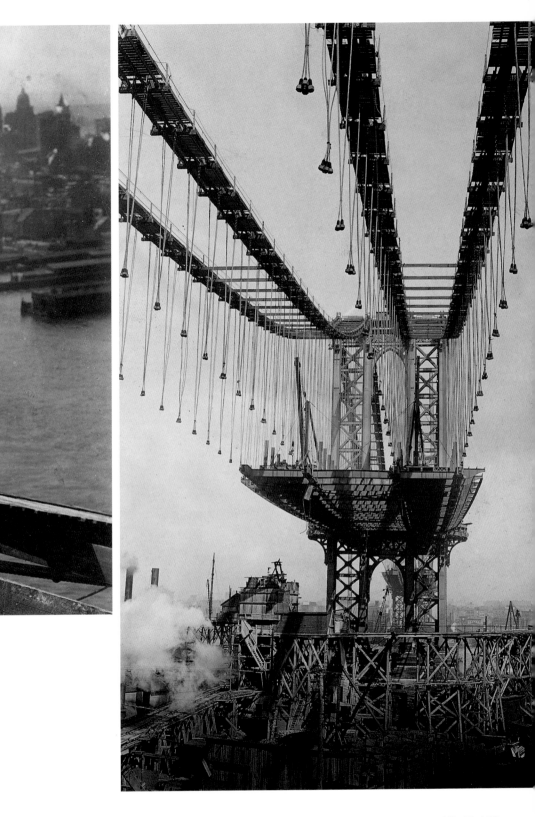

Above: The architectural firm of John Carrère and Thomas Hastings designed
the Manhattan approach to the Manhattan Bridge. They modeled the arch
after Porte St. Denis, one of the gateways to Paris. Inspiration for the colonnade came from the Bernini colonnade at St. Peter's in Rome. Both architects
had trained in Paris at the École des Beaux-Arts and practiced their trade
with McKim, Mead and White prior to breaking out on their own. Perhaps
the pair's most famous commission was the 1897 design for the New York
Public Library at 42nd Street and 5th Avenue.

Below: Multiple forms of transportation—foot, car, and train—are shown in this 1925 photograph of the Manhattan Bridge. The original bridge design included two roadways, four trolley lines, and four elevated railroad tracks in anticipation of traffic demands in the twentieth century.

Opposite: Standing under the Manhattan Bridge at the Bowery and Canal Street, Berenice Abbott captured the elegance of Moisseiff's tower design in this photograph shot on November 11, 1936.

Above: The Manhattan Bridge has a certain rhythmic beauty, as shown in this image also taken on November 11, 1936, by Abbott.

Left: On April 1, 1937, Abbott returned to documenting the Manhattan Bridge, this time on Pike Slip at South Street under the span on the Manhattan side.

Below: The Manhattan Bridge was reconfigured in the 1940s to handle seven lanes of vehicular traffic—four lanes on the upper deck and three lanes on the lower deck, where they replaced the original trolley tracks.

Right: Gustav Lindenthal's Hell Gate Bridge (1916) was sponsored by the Pennsylvania Railroad to connect its lines, which included the Long Island Rail Road, with the New York, New Haven and Hartford Railroad. The bridge is part of a system that includes viaducts, overpasses, and two smaller bridges—the Little Hell Gate and Bronx Kill Bridges—and extends approximately 3.2 miles (5km) from Queens to the Bronx.

Above: Cranes maneuver to position the last steel beams of the Hell Gate Bridge on September 30, 1915. Construction of the bridge was complicated by its location over the narrowest portion of Hell Gate, the East River passage separating Queens from Wards Island that is marked by dangerous currents. Navigation had to be kept open at all times, thereby preventing traditional use of falsework or scaffolding in building the arch. Instead, work began simultaneously from each tower, and the bridge was constructed to join in the middle.

Above: Lindenthal's choice of massive masonry towers for the Hell Gate Bridge was prompted more by artistic consideration than structural need. His preferred choice of steel girders for the viaduct piers was vetoed, because it was feared that patients of the Wards Island Psychiatric Hospital and inmates from the Randall's Island correctional facility might use them for escape. Instead, Lindenthal was required to reconfigure that portion of his design using less appealing solid concrete. Nonetheless, his attention to the placement and proportions of the arch resulted in the bridge's pleasing profile.

Left: Berenice Abbott photographed the Hell Gate Bridge from the Queens neighborhood of Astoria in 1936. When completed, the Hell Gate Bridge, with its four railroad tracks and 1,017-foot (310m) arch, was the longest steel arch bridge in the world. It was also one of the heaviest bridges, said to incorporate more steel than its designer's previous bridge projects—the Manhattan and Queensboro Bridges—combined.

Above: In the process of connecting Queens and the Bronx, the Hell Gate Bridge crosses over Wards Island, an area that has served a number of uses since 1637 when the Dutch purchased the land. Brothers Jasper and Bartholomew Ward farmed on the island after the American Revolution and lent their name to the site. In the 1850s, the city purchased the island and used it for a potter's field, an immigrant station, and a hospital for the destitute, the latter eventually evolving into the Manhattan State Hospital and later the Manhattan Psychiatric Center. During the twentieth century, Wards Island served as home to a sewage treatment facility and a training school for the fire department. Today, much of the island is a public park.

Above: The George Washington Bridge (1931) lights up the nighttime sky over the Hudson River. The illumination not only enhances the beauty of the bridge, but also serves the practical purpose of guiding airplanes flying in the area.

CHAPTER THREE

Twentieth-Century Innovator

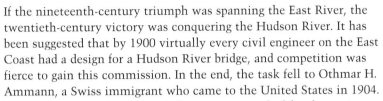

If the nineteenth-century triumph was spanning the East River, the twentieth-century victory was conquering the Hudson River. It has been suggested that by 1900 virtually every civil engineer on the East Coast had a design for a Hudson River bridge, and competition was fierce to gain this commission. In the end, the task fell to Othmar H. Ammann, a Swiss immigrant who came to the United States in 1904.

Upon his arrival in New York, Ammann worked for the engineering firm of Joseph Mayer on lower Broadway. Although he stayed with Mayer for less than a year, Ammann worked on dozens of railroad bridge projects. After a trip to the Palisades in New Jersey, he also began to conceive his own idea for a Hudson River crossing.

After he left Mayer's employ in November 1904, Ammann spent time in both western Pennsylvania and Chicago working for various engineering firms. While employed by the Pennsylvania Steel Company in Harrisburg, Pennsylvania, he worked on one of the company's bigger contracts—the fabrication of the Queensboro Bridge. In 1907, when the Quebec Bridge collapse occurred, he was asked to join Frederick C. Kunz and Charles C. Schneider, designer of the Washington Bridge, as part of the investigation team. Ammann continued his association with the two men when he relocated to Philadelphia to work in the newly created engineering firm Schneider and Kunz. However, by 1912 Ammann was back in New York—this time on Gustav Lindenthal's payroll—and within three months he was appointed chief assistant on the Hell Gate Bridge. By the time of that span's completion in 1916, Ammann was deputy chief engineer. But the entry of the United States into World War I effectively put a stop to all major bridge projects under consideration. There was little, if any, work in Lindenthal's engineering office, and Ammann ended up working as manager of a clay mine—owned by Lindenthal and his partner George Silzer—in South Amboy, New Jersey. He stayed there until the early 1920s, when he returned to New York City in order to assist on Lindenthal's Hudson River crossing.

As early as 1868, the New Jersey State Legislature had authorized the New York and New Jersey Bridge Company to develop a Hudson River crossing for the area near the southern edge of Union township. Throughout the 1870s and 1880s, numerous proposals were offered for review. Gustav Lindenthal was one of the earliest proponents of the Hudson River bridge idea. However, he advocated caution and restraint with regard to the aesthetics of the bridge, as evidenced by his February 4, 1888, thoughts in *Engineering News*: "It is certainly true that if New York Harbor, acknowledged to be the most beautiful in the country, should be defaced by a utility bridge of shabby appearance, it would be an unpardonable offense against the civilization of mankind." In the meantime, public enthusiasm was a driving force, and on July 3, 1888, *The New York Times* proclaimed that "we shall have a bridge across the Hudson into this city ere the century closes." Their prediction was a bit premature, as it would take more time to achieve this goal. Because any Hudson River span would impact both states, a consensus between the two needed to be reached before any work could even begin. It was not until 1890 that New York State passed approval for such a project, with the caveat that any bridge structure created in the Hudson could not include piers obstructing river traffic.

Gustav Lindenthal was ready for what he knew would be the commission of a lifetime. His proposal for a suspension bridge developed for the North River Bridge Company was supported by railroad interests that saw the value of being able to access Manhattan by avoiding the northern route through the Bronx. His original idea was to erect a crossing at West 10th Street in Manhattan, but he later changed the location to West 23rd Street, allowing the bridge to connect directly to Hoboken, New Jersey. In 1890, Lindenthal's design was presented to the U.S. Army Corps of Engineers. At the time of the review, an alternate proposal for a cantilevered design was being put forth by the New York–New Jersey Bridge Commission, with the intent of building the crossing at West 70th Street in Manhattan. The Corps reviewed both concepts and agreed that although the cantilever design was possible, its cost would be prohibitive and therefore it was better to go with a suspension design. Lindenthal was spurred by this conclusion, but unfortunately, the 1890s were a period of economic downturn and his railroad sponsors placed the idea on hold. By 1900, the railroads were losing interest in a bridge project due to the anticipated costs. Instead, they began looking at tunneling under the Hudson River as an alternative means of connecting their routes through New Jersey to Manhattan. The Hudson and Manhattan Railroad completed a set of tunnels in 1908, and two years later, the Pennsylvania Railroad finished a pair of single-track tunnels that terminated at the future Pennsylvania Station, which would be designed by McKim, Mead and White and completed in 1911.

In 1910, New York and New Jersey public planners went back to the drawing board and determined that a crossing at West 179th Street in Manhattan would be the most appropriate place for a Hudson River bridge, given the narrowness of the river at that point. However, test borings revealed that building the foundation for the bridge there would prove just as difficult as at the previously suggested midtown sites. Once again, Gustav Lindenthal came to the joint bridge commission with a design, this time located at Manhattan's West 59th Street. The new proposal came with a price tag of $76 million. But there was an even bigger problem than cost. Lindenthal's solution revolved around nineteenth-century transportation—the railroad.

By emphasizing the design's capacity for sixteen tracks, he failed to realize that the future lay with the automobile. In 1910, there were 458,500 cars registered to individuals throughout the country, and by 1916, the annual production of Ford's Model T was 738,881 units. Any potential Hudson River crossing needed to focus on the requirements of automotive technology.

While Lindenthal was hard at work on his Hudson River railroad bridge concepts, progress continued on alternative crossings—namely tunnels, sometimes called "underwater streets." The success of the railroad excavations in 1910 led to subway tunnels, and by 1919, work had begun under the Hudson on a vehicle tube that would be called the Holland Tunnel. But the problem of automobile congestion was increasing, and more crossings were needed to facilitate access to and from Manhattan. As demand increased, so did the number of players—state, city, federal, county—and there became a need to coordinate the various building projects and proposals. In 1921, the Port of New York Authority was established as a joint public interest by the states of New York and New Jersey in order to improve access to the ports and transportation systems shared by the two. (The name of the agency was changed in 1972 to the Port Authority of New York and New Jersey.) The collaborative effort on the Holland Tunnel had shown that the two states could work together, and the Port Authority took over as the master planner not only for tunnel routes, but also for bridges. It had taken nearly sixty years, but work was finally about to begin on a Hudson River bridge.

When Ammann returned to Lindenthal's firm, the stage was set for conflict. Lindenthal was determined to create a bridge that would connect the area around Manhattan's West 57th Street with Weehawken, New Jersey. Ammann, however, saw the value in a less ambitious project and continued work on his own proposal based on the idea of a span between West 179th Street and Fort Lee, New Jersey. Lindenthal's complete focus on the Hudson River project—now estimated to cost nearly half a billion dollars—to the exclusion of all else caused economic problems for the firm. In late 1922, Ammann was asked to take a pay cut, and by early 1923, his savings were nearly gone. On March 21 of that year, Ammann quit Lindenthal's engineering firm and struck out on his own.

Ammann was headed for a showdown with Lindenthal. In the middle of 1923, using his own letterhead marked "O.H. Ammann, Consulting Engineer," Ammann wrote to George Silzer, who had recently been elected governor of New Jersey, to express his views on various proposals for the Hudson River bridge. Although Ammann expressed "no desire to discredit Mr. Lindenthal," he went on to detail the problems he saw with the Weehawken–57th Street bridge proposal, suggesting an alternative solution based on his own analysis. The Port Authority eventually rejected the Weehawken–57th Street connector for many of the reasons Ammann had identified. Public hearings were scheduled for additional proposals, and Ammann's Fort Lee–179th Street concept was presented. With an estimated cost of $25 million to $30 million, his was a feasible alternative. As a courtesy, Governor Silzer sent a copy of Ammann's proposal to his former business associate, Gustav Lindenthal. The latter replied on December 20, 1923, with a denouncement of Ammann, stating that Ammann's cost estimate was unreasonable and that Ammann had used his position in Lindenthal's firm to gain access to his plans and compete for the Hudson River bridge project. Lindenthal had worked on a Hudson River bridge concept for nearly forty years, only to see it pulled away from him by an assistant. Although Ammann's Hudson River bridge proposal was accepted, he was not immediately involved in the project. For the next eighteen months, he worked on his own. Then, in July 1925, he was hired as bridge engineer for the

Port Authority. In his first year, while he worked on detailing the Hudson River bridge project, Ammann was also busy designing the Bayonne Bridge, which would connect Port Richmond in Staten Island with Bayonne, New Jersey. Construction on the Bayonne project began in 1928 and marked Ammann's first collaboration with architect Cass Gilbert. Upon its completion in 1931, the Bayonne Bridge was the longest steel arch bridge in the world, a record it held until 1977. During his first three years with the Port Authority, Ammann would also oversee two other Staten Island bridge projects—the Goethals Bridge and the Outerbridge Crossing—that had begun prior to his appointment.

In 1927, work finally began on the Hudson River bridge. When completed in 1931, Ammann's masterpiece was the longest steel suspension bridge in the world, its 3,500-foot (1,067m)-long span more than doubling the previous record held by Detroit's Ambassador Bridge (1929). Ammann and architect Gilbert had envisioned granite-sheathed bridge towers, but cost-cutting measures during the first years of the Depression required getting rid of nonessential architectural embellishment. As a result, the bare steel suspension bridge, now called the George Washington Bridge, was the epitome of modern design and a true statement of twentieth-century sensibility when compared to New York City's nineteenth-century bridges. Years later, the great architect Le Corbusier commented on the powerful effect of the George Washington Bridge in his 1947 book *When Cathedrals Were White*: "When your car moves up the ramp the two towers rise so high that it brings you happiness; their structure is so pure, so resolute, so regular, that here, finally, steel architecture seems to laugh...." Le Corbusier's mention of the automobile reflects the direction that New York City's public works projects took during the remainder of the twentieth century. While Ammann's vision with regard to the future of transportation set him apart from Gustav Lindenthal, it gave him something in common with Robert Moses, referred to as "the master builder of twentieth-century New York." Beginning with his 1934 appointment as New York City Parks Commissioner and continuing until 1968 when he stepped down from the Triborough Bridge and Tunnel Authority, Moses would oversee the transformation of New York from a trolley-and-carriage town into an automotive city. Under his supervision, thirteen vehicle bridges and more than four hundred miles (644km) of highway would be constructed, creating a transportation hub that linked New England, Long Island, and the Middle Atlantic states.

Othmar Ammann and Robert Moses began their association with the Triborough Bridge project. One of the city's most ambitious undertakings, the system incorporates three-and-a-half miles (5.5km) of viaduct with three bridges connecting Manhattan, the Bronx, and Queens. Work had begun on October 25, 1929, the day after the "Black Thursday" stock market crash, but was suspended by early 1930 due to the economic downturn.

Opposite: The Harlem River Lift Bridge, one of the three primary spans that make up the Triborough Bridge, nears completion on May 13, 1936. Positioned at East 125th Street, the bridge connects Manhattan with Randall's Island. The "lift" functions similarly to an elevator in that sections of the roadway can be raised or lifted to allow ships to pass underneath. In the case of the Harlem River Lift Bridge, the 310-foot (94.5m)-long center span can be elevated 80 feet (24.4m) to provide 135 feet (41m) of clearance above the river.

Opposite: The elegant Bronx–Whitestone Bridge, which was the fourth longest suspension bridge in the world upon its completion, incorporates the deflection theory utilized in the Manhattan and George Washington Bridges. Subject to sway, the delicate bridge was retrofitted in 1946 with Warren stiffening trusses.

The Triborough Bridge was an abandoned construction site when Robert Moses became involved through his role as chairman of the New York State Emergency Public Works Commission. He came up with the idea of forming the Triborough Bridge and Tunnel Authority as an independent agency and applied for federal funds to jump-start the project. The Triborough Authority received a $37 million loan from the federal government as part of the new Works Progress Administration. Moses enticed Ammann to the project by allowing him to serve as chief engineer while keeping his appointment with the Port Authority. In 1934, Ammann came on board; the project was completed two years later.

Working for Moses allowed Ammann to design another great bridge, the Bronx–Whitestone suspension span. Upon its completion in a record twenty-three months—in time for the 1939 World's Fair—the Bronx–Whitestone Bridge confirmed Ammann's place as one of the twentieth century's great bridge designers. The Bronx–Whitestone Bridge also contributed to development in Queens, and within twenty years, heavy bridge use spurred the construction of an alternate thoroughfare, the Throgs Neck Bridge, which was completed by Ammann in 1961.

Othmar Ammann turned sixty in 1939. After fourteen years with the Port Authority, he returned to private practice and formed a new company with landscape architect Charles C. Combs. In 1941, Ammann was appointed to a federal team investigating the failure of the Tacoma Narrows Bridge designed by Leon S. Moisseiff, creator of the Manhattan Bridge. While his findings exonerated Moisseiff, Ammann did report on issues of instability that forced him to retro-fit his own Bronx–Whitestone Bridge with stiffening trusses in 1946. Upon his son Werner's return from service in World War II, Ammann and Combs merged with a Midwest company to create Ammann and Whitney, Consulting Engineers—one of the first national civil engi-neering firms. Throughout the 1950s and 1960s, this new company received all the design work for long-span bridge projects in the New York City area. In addition to the aforementioned Throgs Neck Bridge, Ammann and Whitney completed the expansion of the George Washington Bridge in 1962.

Ammann's last major project was the design and construction of the Verrazano Narrows Bridge, begun in September 1959 and completed five years later in November 1964. When this suspension bridge—which connects Staten Island and Brooklyn—was finished, it returned the "world's longest bridge" crown to New York, albeit only until 1981. The bridge is an aesthetic masterpiece, what Robert Moses referred to as a "triumph of simplicity and restraint."

Today, more than two thousand bridges serve New York City. These structures carry people and vehicles over both land and water. Some are simple pedestrian walkways within the city's vast park system. Others are engineering marvels that demonstrate the juncture of design and technology. All, however, share a common purpose—to overcome physical barriers and join people together.

Above: Originally, Othmar Ammann wanted to sheath the two towers of the George Washington Bridge (1931) with granite. But the financial conditions of the 1930s dictated a more modest construction. The resulting exposed steel towers offer a stark beauty in keeping with modern design.

Opposite, top: This photograph from 1929 shows the construction phase of stringing cable for the George Washington Bridge. The contractor for this portion of the project was John A. Roebling and Sons, the cable wire manufacturer founded by John Roebling, creator of the Brooklyn Bridge (1883). Completion of the bridge required an estimated 107,000 miles (172,163km) of steel cable wire weighing an estimated 28,100 tons (25,487t).

Above: A worker pauses along the catwalk of the George Washington Bridge, where bundles of cable strands are ready for spinning into the supporting suspension cables. Each of the main cables required 61 cable strands—with each strand containing 434 individual wires.

Left: A laborer works atop one of the George Washington Bridge's towers. Note the suspender cables hanging from the main cable at left. These would be used to attach the road deck during the next stage of construction. The foreground of this image shows the rivet construction used to hold the tower sections together. An estimated 475,000 rivets were required to complete each tower.

Below: This image suggests that workmen used a wire harness system to cross over the Hudson River during the early construction phase of the George Washington Bridge.

Above: A single tower of the George Washington Bridge awaits the addition of suspender cables. The catwalks, which appear to be very close to the main cables in this photograph, are actually hanging four feet (1m) below them. In the 1930s, these towers were taller than most of the high-rise construction under way in midtown Manhattan. Each tower contains an estimated twenty thousand tons (18,140t) of steel and soars more than six hundred feet (183m) above the river's surface.

Above: In order to construct the roadway approach to the George Washington Bridge on the Manhattan side, a substantial amount of demolition work was required within the Fort Washington Park neighborhood. Approximately six blocks were cleared. Once the approach was in service, traffic patterns had minimal impact on the area, as the primary on and off ramps lead to Riverside Drive.

Opposite, bottom: A woman looks out over the Hudson River as she stands between two of the four cables that hold the George Washington Bridge hundreds of feet above the water. This 1949 image provides a sense of the tremendous size of the primary bridge supports. In designing the bridge, Othmar Ammann utilized deflection theory—first tested by Leon Moisseiff in his design of the Manhattan Bridge (1909)—arguing that as the weight per linear foot increases on a bridge, the requirement for stiffening reinforcement decreases because the structure's own deadweight contributes to its stability. He also experimented with the use of plate girders on the underside of the roadway rather than employing the traditional method of stiffening truss work.

Above: Crowds line the Manhattan roadway plaza of the George Washington Bridge on October 24, 1931, the span's dedication day. Naming a bridge is serious business and although George Washington Memorial Bridge ended up being the official title—later shortened to George Washington Bridge—other names came under consideration during the planning process. The Port Authority invited suggestions from the public, and the possibilities included "Palisades Bridge," "Fort Lee Bridge," "Columbus Bridge," and even "Verrazano Bridge."

Above: Although the George Washington Bridge was a twentieth-century accomplishment, its dedication day reflected the jubilant celebrations of its nineteenth-century predecessors. More than five thousand invited guests sat in the bleachers that stretched the entire length of the bridge, while crowds jammed the Manhattan and New Jersey toll plazas. In addition to a military parade, thirty-five planes flew in formation overhead.

Below: New York governor Franklin D. Roosevelt shakes hands with New Jersey governor Morgan F. Larson. Many other dignitaries were also in attendance at the opening ceremonies for the George Washington Bridge. The dedication speeches were broadcast to the crowds standing in the Manhattan and New Jersey toll plazas, as well as transmitted live on the radio.

Above: Cars line up at the New Jersey toll plaza of the George Washington Bridge on opening day. The impressive structure held the title of world's longest suspension bridge until 1937, when San Francisco's Golden Gate Bridge—with a span of 4,200 feet (1,280m)—captured the title.

Right: Cars heading toward Manhattan find themselves in a massive traffic jam at the New Jersey approach of the George Washington Bridge on October 25, 1931, the span's first full day of operation. According to the records, 56,312 cars were counted on that first day, a hint of rush hours to come.

Left: The George Washington Bridge was designed for the automobile. When the crossing first opened, there were six motor vehicle lanes and two lanes reserved for pedestrians and bicycles. The center lane of the bridge was originally planned for subway or trolley traffic, as shown in this 1930s image, but it was left empty until 1946, when it was paved over for two additional motor vehicle lanes. By the 1950s, eight lanes were not enough to handle the heavy traffic on the bridge, and construction began on a lower deck, which added another six lanes in 1962.

Left, top: Othmar Ammann (left) reviews plans for the addition of a lower deck to the George Washington Bridge. Ammann was in his late seventies at the time.

Left, bottom: Construction work progresses on the concrete foundation of the new six-lane lower deck for the George Washington Bridge. The addition cost nearly three times the budget of the original bridge.

Opposite: This dramatic photograph, taken on October 27, 1955, shows an unusual sight—the George Washington Bridge deserted during rush hour. The absence of cars was due to an air raid drill in New Jersey, which put a stop to all traffic.

Left: Othmar Ammann also designed the Bayonne Bridge (1931). It is one of three Staten Island bridges finished under his supervision as chief engineer for the Port Authority, the other two being the Goethals Bridge and the Outerbridge Crossing—both completed in 1928. Prior to the construction of these bridges, the only land link Staten Island had was a circa 1890 railroad bridge over the Arthur Kill, a tidal strait separating the New York City borough from New Jersey. All of the aforementioned crossings were created to connect Staten Island with New Jersey. It would be another thirty years before a Staten Island–Brooklyn connector was built.

Left, top: Workers oversee cable spinning on the East River Suspension Bridge of the Triborough Bridge. The groundbreaking for the entire project occurred on October 25, 1929—the day after the stock market crashed. Work continued into early 1930 before the city ran out of funding. At that point, only the anchorage and tower foundations were finished. The project sat idle for nearly two years before work resumed.

Left, bottom: This unusual angle shows workers on one of the towers of the Triborough's East River Suspension Bridge, which crosses Hell Gate to connect Astoria, Queens, with Wards Island. With a span of 1,380 feet (420.5m), the suspension bridge is longer than the Queensboro Bridge but slightly shorter than the other East River crossings. It is this particular span that comes to mind when most people think of the Triborough Bridge.

Opposite: The towers of the Triborough's East River Suspension Bridge reflect the aesthetic sensibilities that guided Ammann in his design of the George Washington Bridge. (The original tower design, before Ammann's involvement, mirrored the gothic feel of the Brooklyn Bridge.)

Right: The towers of the Harlem River Lift Bridge have a utilitarian look that contrasts with the elegant towers Ammann designed for the East River Suspension Bridge. The lift bridge's towers perform a more complex duty than merely holding up the structure. Inside the towers are the electric motors used to hoist the center deck above the river to allow ships to pass.

Left: The Triborough Bridge opened on July 11, 1936, in the middle of a heat wave. Despite the oppressive weather, nearly 15,000 people gathered for the celebration and another 200,000 crossed the Triborough during its first twenty-four hours in operation.

Left: President Franklin D. Roosevelt speaks at the dedication ceremonies for the Triborough Bridge on Randall's Island. Sitting at left are New York City mayor Fiorello H. La Guardia and New York governor Herbert H. Lehman.

Right: Berenice Abbott photographed the East 125th Street approach from Manhattan onto the Triborough's Harlem River Lift Bridge on June 29, 1937—about a year after its opening.

Below: Placement of the Harlem River Lift Bridge involved good old-fashioned New York City politics. Robert Moses's preference was to locate the Manhattan tower at East 103rd Street so that the connecting tower on Randall's Island would not interfere with the grounds of state facilities located there. But he was pressured to accept an East 125th Street location on properties owned by the Hearst family's real estate interests. Moses reluctantly agreed to the site, as he felt that arguing the point would result in cancellation of the project.

Opposite: As the suspension portion of the Triborough Bridge crosses overhead, people relax on Wards Island.

Left: The Triborough Bridge is a beautiful addition to the evening landscape, as shown in this 1967 photograph by Peter Fink.

Above: The Throgs Neck Bridge was one of the last designs by Othmar Ammann. The steel suspension bridge opened on July 11, 1961, to alleviate traffic on the popular Bronx–Whitestone Bridge, which was carrying an estimated 33.2 million vehicles per year by 1960. The bridge spans the meeting point of the East River and Long Island Sound, connecting Throgs Neck in the Bronx and Bayside in Queens. In this image, a bicycle rider sneaks across the bridge prior to its official opening. By 1966, an estimated annual 30 million vehicles were using the Throgs Neck Bridge.

Left: Workers lay cable on the Verrazano Narrows Bridge (1964). The four main suspension cables are approximately 36 inches (91.5cm) in diameter and can support a weight load 75 percent greater than that of San Francisco's Golden Gate Bridge.

Above: The road deck of the Verrazano Narrows Bridge was built off-site and lifted into place in 66 preassembled steel sections, each of which weighs 400 tons (363t). The double-deck roadway hangs 228 feet (69.5m) above the water, giving ships more than enough clearance to enter New York Harbor. The bridge has 12 lanes and can carry an annual capacity of 48 million vehicles.

Above: Steelworkers join preassembled sections of the roadway for the Verrazano Narrows Bridge. Many of these workers were local veterans of Manhattan's skyscraper industry. Others were "boomers," the itinerant laborers who moved from bridge project to bridge project. And some were members of the Mohawk people, who commuted from northern New York State to the city every week.

Opposite: The workers pictured here are just a few of the estimated twelve thousand who helped construct the Verrazano Narrows Bridge. Bridge work is dangerous business and the Verrazano Narrows project was no exception. Construction accidents claimed the lives of three men during the course of the project. As a result of the third death—which occurred when a young man fell from the catwalk during cable spinning—safety nets were installed, saving the lives of four men who fell during the remaining work on the bridge.

Below: This photograph shows the official motorcade traveling across the Verrazano Narrows Bridge during the opening ceremony on November 21, 1964. Othmar Ammann was present to hear Robert Moses, chairman of the Triborough Bridge and Tunnel Authority, attribute Ammann's contributions as belonging to "the greatest living bridge engineer, perhaps the greatest of all time," without ever mentioning his name.

Opposite: A luxury liner passes underneath the newly opened Verrazano Narrows Bridge. The completed bridge used 188,000 tons (170,516t) of steel—three times the amount used in the Empire State Building. With a main span of 4,260 feet (1,298m)—13,700 feet (4,176m) including the approaches—and a total weight of 1,265,000 tons (1,147,355t), the span was the world's longest and heaviest suspension bridge when it opened in 1964. The bridge held on to its title until 1981, when the mantle was passed to the Humber Bridge in Hull, England. Today, the record is held by Japan's Akashi Kaikyo Bridge, completed in 1998, with a span of 6,529 feet (1,990m)—more than four times the length of the Brooklyn Bridge.

Sources

BOOKS

Numerous books have been written about New York City and its bridges. The following publications were used in the research for this book and may prove interesting for further reading:

Bascove, Mary Gordon. *Stone and Steel: Paintings and Writings Celebrating the Bridges of New York City*. Boston: David R. Grove, 1998.

Bennett, David. *The Creation of Bridges*. Edison, N.J.: Chartwell Books, 1999.

Dupre, Judith. *Bridges*. New York: Black Dog & Leventhal Publishers, 1997.

Flink, James J. *The Automobile Age*. Cambridge, Mass.: The MIT Press, 1988.

Hindle, Brooke, and Steven Lubar. *Engines of Change: The American Industrial Revolution, 1790–1860*. Washington, D.C.: Smithsonian Institution Press, 1986.

Jackson, Kenneth T., ed. *The Encyclopedia of New York City*. New Haven, Conn.: Yale University Press, 1995.

Le Corbusier. *When the Cathedrals Were White*. New York: Reynal & Hitchcock, 1947.

Miller, Donald L., ed. *The Lewis Mumford Reader*. New York: Pantheon Books, 1986.

Petroski, Henri. *Engineers of Dreams: Great Bridge Builders and the Spanning of America*. New York: Vintage Books, 1995.

Pope, Thomas. *A Treatise on Bridge Architecture*. New York: A. Niven, 1811.

Pursell, Carroll. *The Machine in America: A Social History of Technology*. Baltimore: The Johns Hopkins University Press, 1995.

Rastorfer, Darl. *Six Bridges: The Legacy of Othmar H. Ammann*. New Haven: Yale University Press, 2000.

Reier, Sharon. *The Bridges of New York*. Mineola, N.Y.: Dover Publications, Inc., 1977.

Stilgoe, John R. *Common Landscape of America, 1580 to 1845*. New Haven: Yale University Press, 1982.

WEBSITES

In addition to traditional reference materials, there are numerous websites offering information. The following sites are good starting points:

www.bronxhistoricalsociety.org
The Bronx County Historical Society

www.brooklynhistory.org
The Brooklyn Historical Society

www.loc.gov
The Library of Congress

www.mta.nyc.ny.us
Metropolitan Transportation Authority

www.mcny.org
The Museum of the City of New York

www.nyc.gov/html/dot
New York City Department of Transportation

www.nycroads.com
New York City Roads

www.nyhistory.org
The New-York Historical Society

www.nypl.org
New York Public Library

www.panynj.gov
The Port Authority of New York and New Jersey

Index

Photo Credits